The first condition of success is that if you read one or two chapters of this book and make your mindset that this book is useless for you, then you are not ready to become a successful author. The second condition to become a successful author is to read the book completely and then give your opinion. I am confident that this book will change your thinking and help you become a best-selling author.

HOW TO BECOME BEST SELLER AUTHOR?

RAJENDER SINGH BISHT

Title	:	How to Become Best Seller Author
Author	:	Rajender Singh Bisht
Edition	:	1st (January, 2024)
ISBN	:	9789387856905

Published by

PRACHI
DIGITAL PUBLICATION

Regd. Add.	:	254, Khuriyakhatta No. 10, Bindukhatta, Lalkuan, Nainital - 262402, Uttarakhand, India
Website	:	www.prachidigital.com
E-mail	:	info@prachidigital.in
Phone	:	+91 976041 7980
		+91 976041 8103

INDEX

Why this book?

Every writer dreams that his name is included in the list of best selling authors. It is a different matter that some writers want to become a best seller to earn money, while some writers want to become a best seller just to make a name. Now it depends on you with which mindset you want to become a best seller. But often this question always looms like a deer in the mind of every new writer or the writers who have published a book, how to become a best seller or why we could not become a best seller or what is missing in our writing. Due to which we could not become successful writers.

'How to become a best seller?' If you search this sentence on Google, you will get to read many articles in the Google search results, in which you will be told what to write, how to write, how to publish a book, how to choose a publisher, the process of becoming a writer. , giving you tips for writing and a lot of information related to how to do marketing etc., but all the articles obtained from the search results do not tell you many important things which are important for all writers to know. So that the author has all these important information in advance and the author can create his mindset or prepare a blue print for the success of his book.

In this book, a small attempt has been made to explain how to become a best seller or the reasons why you are not able to become a best seller author. Apart from this, many important information is also given in the book for the writers, which every writer should know, because many times writers fail to become successful writers due to lack of sufficient information. After which many times writers remain regretful throughout their life that they could not become successful writers, but why? They are unable to figure out this point throughout their life. Being in the publishing business, I have tried to know the writers very closely, the result of which is this book, so that I can help the writers become successful through this book.

If you go to online book stores or offline markets and search for books to become a writer, you will find a lot of books of 200-400 pages to read, which will teach you how to become a writer. Apart from this, in the digital age, many successful writers are also running online classes to become best selling writers. But it is worth noting that you can become a writer by taking their classes or reading books like how to become a successful writer, but you cannot create your mindset for success. For that, you need to know yourself as well as the publishing industry to see if you are ready to become a best-selling author.

A lot of care has been taken in the book that boring articles should not be included in the book and instead of making the book too big, only the necessary information and articles have been included. Due to which this book may seem small to you, because an attempt has been made to give a lot of information in few words. It is also noteworthy that no one wants to read a very long book.

If you are a published author but have not been able to become a best seller, you will find your mistakes in this book. If you are a new writer then you can create a mindset for your success by reading this book. If you read and follow this book carefully, you may be the next best seller. I have full confidence that this book will help new and published writers to become best selling authors.

Your Sincerely
Rajender Singh Bisht

<u>Chapter 1</u>

Be Ready to take Risks and Become a Best Seller

If you are a writer who wants to become a best selling author and you are ready to work hard and struggle, then this book is going to be a profitable deal for you. First of all, I want to tell you that for our success it is necessary for us to work hard and struggle, only then we can be successful. Lord Buddha has also given the same message in short words -

App Deepo Bhav.

That is, Lord Buddha has said in his message that instead of expecting from someone else, be your own light (inspiration). No one can pave the way for anyone's success. A person should decide the purpose of his life himself. You should not expect your success from anyone else.

If you want to become a successful author then you have to work for yourself and find your own path to success, because no one will give their time or take risks for your success. Therefore, instead of blaming other people for your failure, try for your success, and keep trying continuously, leaving aside the dream of becoming successful depending on others. You can achieve success only through your continuous efforts.

I was reading a famous book 'Rich Dad Poor Dad' which gave me a very inspiring message in which most of the people blame others for their failure. As most of the employees work just so that they can remain on the job or get a good salary.

At the same time, many employees, while working in their own company or factory, blame their owner or boss for paying less or being used by their owner or boss. Whereas these are the employees who do not work to enhance their qualifications nor do they have any such plans in the future, they keep blaming their boss or boss on a daily basis and will continue to do so, but still their company or They keep working at the workplace because they have to work just to survive.

They are afraid to strive for their own success, because the fear of losing their job prevents them from taking the time to pursue success or being motivated to learn something new. In this way such employees keep working continuously throughout their life without any purpose. They do not know what their purpose is in their life. They aimlessly wake up every day in the morning and get ready and go to office or workplace, then come home in the evening and then go to sleep. Following this routine, they then wait for the end of the month, because on that day they wait for their salary.

The author of 'Rich Dad Poor Dad' has written in his book that if such employees consider their boss or company owner responsible for their condition, then they will have to change their boss or company owner.

If you hold yourself responsible for your dissatisfaction, change yourself and learn something new. According to the book 'Rich Dad Poor Dad', most of the people in the world want to change everyone's mentality as per their own, while they do not want to change themselves or do not want to learn anything new. It is also worth mentioning that it is easier to change yourself than changing others. So stop blaming others for your failure or problem and work for yourself.

Even if such employees do not change themselves and look for a new job with a better salary or promotion, it will never reduce their problems because they will find their boss everywhere not doing justice to them, because This unjust fact has made its home in his mind. They have developed the mentality that their boss or other people are responsible for their failure or dissatisfaction. Apart from this, such people want to work only for money, for them only money is important. Due to which they are never able to achieve a successful life and keep running for money all their life. If you want to achieve money in your life, then the first condition is to be successful and keep learning continuously.

I have noticed in most of the cases that most of the authors also make such mistakes. It is worth noting that most of the authors do not want to work for themselves, due to which they blame publishers for their failure and thus remain unsuccessful throughout their life.

You must have often seen such families making their living, who are living in extreme poverty. Keeping their lifestyle in mind, people of the society often say that a person who does not work for his own success cannot come out of poverty. Do you know why they are poor? Because they never think about their success, because their first aim is to earn money just for today, so that they can eat bread in the evening. Because of which they do not think about the future. The same rule works with authors too, because most authors are not conscious of their future, they only want to achieve success today and with immediate impact. They want to earn money in the form of royalty without doing their hard work. Due to which most of the authors fail in their life.

I have often noticed that many times authors negotiate royalties with a self-publishing publisher for the sole purpose of making money, or just for the satisfaction of getting the book published, they forget to work for their own success. In most of the cases authors never think about their own success, they just hustle to earn money in the form of royalties. You can learn or take the message by reading the biographies of successful people that if you become successful in life, money follows you, you do not need to rush or bargain for money.

Often authors say that our job is only to write, which we have already done, the work beyond this is the responsibility of the publisher. But have you ever asked yourself – do you want to become a successful author or a best seller author? This means that you are writing only to get the book published or have you written only to become a published author?

If you want to become a successful author in your life, you have to change your mindset. You have to create the mindset that you really have to become a successful author, only then you can make your name in the list of successful authors. If you think that my work is limited to writing and the publisher's job is to publish and make the writer a best selling author, then there is no chance of you becoming a successful author, because you do not have the passion to become a successful author. That is, you do not want to take any risks or put in the effort for your success. Here I would like to say that history is witness to the fact that those people who have worked for their success by taking risks and ignoring the ridicule of the society, have also enjoyed success.

Often authors say that we are not businessmen, we cannot get our manuscript published by paying money, because we do not want to sell what we have written. Such authors should ask themselves why are you writing and why do you want to get your book published? Apart from this, the author also says that he does not find it appropriate to promote his own book, nor does he want to promote his book himself. Whereas it is worth noting that this mentality prevents the writer from becoming a successful author. Because of which such authors always wait for a publisher who can take the risk to publish their book. Whereas such authors never get success in their entire life, due to which their dream remains unfulfilled and they are not able to be included in the count of successful authors.

Many times it is the luck of the author or some authors are successful in getting their book published traditionally due to their friends and colleagues having direct contact with traditional publishers, but still they are not able to become successful authors.

While it is worth noting that through such contacts his book only gets printed, while his book gets published traditionally in the eyes of the world including his family and friends (this regard has been discussed in the following pages). They do not get success even then, because they do not do anything for success, or they do not even want to make some efforts for success, because they do not find it appropriate to work for their book.

I have a respected author friend, I would not like to name him here, who often criticized publishers working on the self-publishing model. Although I was also running a self-publishing company, there was never any argument between us on this matter. He was always in favor of traditional book publishing.

It was his effort or luck that he found a traditional publisher to publish his book, but do you also want to know whether my author friend could become a best-selling author? As far as I know, he is now anonymous because he too did not work for his success and his traditional publisher printed his book and made it available online. It is worth noting that the publisher of his book is not a well-known traditional publisher with the facility of a large distribution network. In this way his book was published free of cost under the traditional model, which was his dream cherished for many years. The working style of traditional publishers providing such services is discussed in subsequent chapters.

The point to consider is that if a author is not willing to put in the effort himself for his success, then why would anyone make the effort for him? Even my personal experience is that success is never achieved without one's own hard work. To climb the final ladder of success, one has to work hard without seeing the difference of day and night.

If you want to become a successful author then you have to change your mindset. Let me tell you that if you create the mindset that your book is your product, then no one can stop you from becoming a successful author. Most importantly, you have to present your book as a product and become a salesman for your book. If you do not want to become a salesman then how will you be able to sell your book or tell others about your book. Therefore, the first condition to become a best selling author is that you have to come out of the mindset of a author and think from the mindset of a salesman or a successful seller.

Look at a businessman, how many mediums he promotes to sell his product and works on many marketing and promotion strategies, after all these efforts he is able to get customers. He plans strategies to sell his product and finds his potential customers. He makes every possible effort to satisfy his customers, so that he can make his business profitable.

Similarly, the author also has to come out of the mindset of a author and realize his book as his product. The way Indian best-selling author Amish Tripathi did not give up even after his manuscript was rejected by many traditional publishing houses. After that Amish self-published his book and made every possible effort to promote it.

It is sad that most of the authors in our country are not aware of the self-publishing model, or the authors try to ignore it despite knowing it. I was reading an article by a author Rajeev Roshan, according to his article, Indians never want to be aware. Indians create a Lakshman Rekha for themselves that we do not want to move beyond this nor listen to anything, then how will they know about these new publishing models and printing technologies.

Just think, what would have happened if the famous Indian author Amish Tripathi had got frustrated and not published his first book under the self-published model and locked it in a cupboard? Imagine if British author E. L. James had not self-published 'Fifty Shades of Grey', would the world have ever been able to read such successful books.

It is noteworthy that if Amish Tripathi had thought about his book from a author's point of view or had developed the mentality that he was just a author and would have just waited for the offer from a traditional publisher, then perhaps no one would have known him today. They would have become somewhere anonymous and would have been living a normal everyday life like other people.

Today, publishers are attracted by their success and give them publishing offers with good royalty, so that they get their new book published first. Whereas in his initial days the publishers had refused to publish his book, and in the end the publisher who decided to publish his book wanted to change his entire story as per his own. Due to which Amish Tripathi took a step towards self-publishing and published the entire book as per his wish and worked for its promotion and marketing. He risked everything - money, mind and time - for the promotion of his book, as a result of which today Amish Tripathi's name is included among the most read authors in India.

Have you ever asked yourself, can I become the next best-selling author? If you haven't done so then question yourself and analyze your own shortcomings. Analyze why you are not able to become a best-selling author. I say that if you change your mindset, you too can become a best-selling author. No obstacle can stop you from becoming a best selling author. The condition is that you work on yourself and make continuous efforts to establish yourself.

I know many authors who have published their books through self-publishing, but they find it disrespectful to discuss their book among friends or acquaintances. They realize that discussing their book on their own is a very bad experience.

It is worth thinking that if a businessman or shopkeeper does not discuss about his product or feels hesitant, then how will people know about his products. Now think for yourself, if I have written a book, then why should I feel ashamed or hesitant, whereas while discussing about my book, I or you should be proud, because if the author himself will not be proud of his book, then how will the potential reader know about your book? Might consider reading the book.

You can also say that to become a best-selling author, you have to make your mindset like that of a businessman or salesman. Don't worry about what people will say, or what will be said about you behind your back. I am repeating the point again that if you look at the history, only those people have been successful in history, who were ridiculed not only behind their back but also in front of them for their innovative experiments or efforts, but today they are successful and their products are sold in their name.

It is also noteworthy that now people imitate him and are becoming successful in the work for which he was once made fun of. So work for yourself, work for your own success and eliminate or ignore the fear of what people will say.

I want to tell you an incident that a person was made fun of for his idea of selling water, but today the same person is selling water to the whole world. Today his company is the number #1 company in the world, with its presence all over the world. If the founder of the water company had stopped his work due to the fear of being ridiculed by the society, his company would hardly have become such a big brand in the world today. For more information about this company, search on Google, you will get complete information.

It is sure that a author can never succeed due to the fear of what people will say or people will make fun of. The decision is in your hands whether you really want to become a successful author or you just want to get your book published?

Always keep in mind that if you want to become a truly successful author in your life, then you will have to make efforts yourself, because if you do not make efforts for your success, then no one in this world will make efforts for your success.

You also have to accept that there is no other alternative to hard work and effort available in this world. There is no short or easy path to success. Without effort and hard work you can never achieve success.

You should not be discouraged by failure despite your efforts. Therefore you should keep in mind that hard work and patience are the basic mantras of success in life. A person can achieve his goal not only through the desires of the mind but also through hard work and continuous effort. That means the only way to success is hard work and continuous efforts.

If you have too many unhelpful excuses to avoid trying to become a successful author. This means that you want to become a successful author but are afraid to take the effort and risk.

Success and not taking risks or not striving for success can never go together. Some authors only dream of being successful, while some authors strive for their success and work hard for it. As a result, those who try become successful and wave the flag of success in the world.

If you really want to become a successful author, then you should always keep in mind that the more difficult your efforts and struggle will be for success, success will also be equally high and glorious. This statement is universally accepted that if you give up or do not want to try for success then no power in the world can make you successful, hence it is said, 'Man ke haare haar hai aur man ke jeete jeet'.

Chapter 2

Take Responsibility for Promoting Your Book

It is often seen that most of the authors think that our job is only to write. We are working hard by devoting a lot of our time, which we have done and the publisher's job is to publish, along with that everything that the author can imagine including selling, marketing, promoting the book. Which is a completely wrong mindset, that is, you are relying on God that only God can help you. Whereas God also helps those who take risks for themselves.

If you have written anything, you are its author, you are the owner of your book, your book is your product. Any hesitation to discuss your product means you don't want to be a successful author, or you don't have the ability to be a successful author. To achieve success, instead of feeling ashamed or hesitant about your book, you should be proud of your book and be responsible for its promotion. Always keep in mind that success is never achieved just by waiting for success or relying on the reversal of fortunes.

Suppose, you want to eat food, then first of all you will have to arrange food items for cooking, and then you will have to make preparations. Then it will have to be cooked and only then you will be able to eat the food. It is not that we will start eating food directly. Similarly, it is easy to become a successful author, but for that you have to prepare your own mindset.

I have observed the mentality of authors for the last several years, under which I have found that most of the authors also have the mentality that if their writing or book is good, then readers will find it themselves. Many times authors say that if their book is good then it will automatically reach the readers. But such authors never think that how will readers find their book? Or how an author's book will reach his potential reader without any effort.

Suppose you cook very good food, which makes anyone lick their fingers, but you will not tell anyone about the dish you have prepared, or will not share your dish with anyone. So how will other people know that you cook very tasty food? Unless you tell someone about your dish, how will anyone know about your dish and your cooking skills?

The same rule applies to your book also. Unless you tell anyone about your book, how will your book be sold? Your book will continue to exist and wait for its readers on the online ecommerce website. You will end up with the mindset that maybe you don't know how to write, or your book was not liked by the readers. In such a situation, you will stop writing or believe that you can never succeed or hold your publisher responsible for the non-sale of your book. That is, you will have to tell people about your book and promote it yourself for your book to be successful.

An astrologer had told me that I would get a government job, but till date I have not applied for a government job because I did not want to do the job. Have I got a government job? The answer to this is no, because I never tried for a government job in my life, nor did I ever make any preparation for a government job. Due to which I never got a government job. Tell me whether without any effort the government itself will come to me and say that your astrologer has said that you will do a government job, hence you are being invited for a government job.

That is, you can believe that unless we make efforts for our success, success will not come to us. Success never comes to us on its own; efforts and hard work are necessary to achieve it. If you want readers for your book, you will have to make efforts, only then your book will be able to reach the readers.

According to a UNESCO report, 90,000 books were published in India in the year 2013. You must know that in the year 2013, the self-publishing model was not as popular as it is today. Note that self-publishing model is most popular among authors today and very affordable self-publishing services are available in the market. Now you can estimate yourself how many millions of books are currently published and how your book will be able to find its readers among these millions of books without any effort.

Always keep in mind that if you feel hesitant in promoting your book or selling it in the bookstores of your city, then you can never become a best-selling author. Moreover, if you want to get your book published only through traditional publishing and not through self-publishing, then you are not doing justice to your dream of becoming a best-selling author or even Maybe you are not serious about the success of your book.

You may have many unwanted reasons for choosing the path of traditional publishing, which may be as follows, the list of which is given below. It is possible that some of these reasons may be yours too-

1. You feel shy or hesitant in promoting or discussing your book among your friends, office colleagues and relatives.

2. Writing a book is just your hobby or you are writing a book just to earn name, so you do not want to invest your own money in publishing the book.

3. You also think that the work of a author is limited to just writing, which you have already done, so you do not want to publish your book through self-publishing.

4. You are not confident in the success of your book, so you want to avoid self-promotion, wasting your time and self-investment.

5. You want to earn money by getting your first book published through a traditional publisher and becoming a best seller, so that after the success of your book, other publishers themselves come to you with offers.

Have you ever observed the daily routine of a vegetable vendor? A vegetable seller goes from street to street selling vegetables. You must be aware that the vegetable vendor does not go to sell vegetables directly. First of all he has to wake up early in the morning and go to the market. He goes to the market and buys vegetables, then returns to his home and sorts the vegetables. After sorting, he decorates the vegetable stall, then he calls out from street to street to sell the vegetables and roams around the streets the whole day, trying to sell all his vegetables.

Suppose, a vegetable seller stands a vegetable cart at a place and rests comfortably and thinks that the one who needs vegetables will come to his cart and buy it. Just think, will his vegetables be sold? You are thinking right, the vegetables of the vegetable seller will not be sold at all, because every day many vegetable sellers roam around in the same streets and make every possible effort to sell their vegetables.

Same is the situation in the world of authors, thousands of books are published every day. The biggest thing is that due to the digital revolution, there is a author or poet in every locality and all of them wish that the publisher should publish their book for free. No publisher should ask them for a single rupee for publication, because they also have the same mentality that writing is our right and it is the responsibility of the publisher to publish for free. Due to this mentality, many times such authors argue with self-publishing publishers and do not get any positive results.

The author's right to free publication, traditional publishing model and self-publishing model are discussed in detail in the subsequent chapters.

It is understandable that if a author himself does not believe in the success of his book, then why would any publisher want to invest money on such authors and why would any reader like to read the book? If you're confident in your book, skip the trips to traditional publishers' offices, self-publish your own book, or have copies of your book printed through a local printer and make new plans for selling and promoting the book. Request help from your friends, family and relatives in promoting your book. Instead of focusing only on earning money in the form of royalties, try to get the book into as many hands as possible.

If you promote your book so much through your own efforts that your name gets included in the list of contemporary authors. Even if your name is at number one thousand in the list of best selling authors, it will be your own success. After this success, if you go to any traditional publisher with a proposal to publish your book, then they may consider investing their money on your book. It is possible that the key to your destiny may open from here.

If you really want your book to be successful then start telling people about your book yourself. After all, if you won't do the marketing for your own book, how can you expect any other organization or individual to help promote your book or do the publicity for you?

Consider getting your book published as a big achievement and it should be something that you should be proud of that your book is published and it is your universal right to promote it with enthusiasm. For example, if a person starts going to the gym, he tells his friends, acquaintances and everyone he knows that I have started going to the gym. Second example, if you go somewhere, then you must share your photo on social media or WhatsApp status, so that your acquaintances and friends can know that you have gone for a trip. Third example, suppose a person buys a new car, then the first thing he tries to tell his friends and relatives is that he has bought a new car. For this, he keeps updating his status on social media or WhatsApp from time to time.

Similarly, if you promote your book well yourself, you will be surprised that it can give a big boost to the sales of your book and people start recognizing you.

Word of mouth has always been the best option for marketing. Let's say you tell your friends about your book and your friends tell their friends and their friends tell other friends, and that's how word of mouth marketing begins. Apart from this, there are many tips through which you can promote your book, for which you will have to find new options yourself.

Chapter 3

Listen to your Heart to Become a Best Seller

It is often seen that some published authors try to mislead new authors by saying this. For example, our books are published free of cost, free publication is the right of the author, the job of the publisher is to publish the author's book without any fee, the job of the publisher is to publish the book and make it available to the readers. Apart from this, many fabricated false stories are told, which often seem true to the authors and directly settle down in the brain.

Apart from this, I have often found authors saying that they are confused about the things they have heard. Through what medium should the author get his book published or should he get his book published by paying a fee or should it be published free of cost? If I am a author then my book should be published free of cost. Many such misconceptions reside in the author's mind, due to which when the author takes advice from other previously published authors, he often accepts what he has heard as true.

I have noticed that in many cases, published authors tell new authors that till now our books have been published for free and due to which we are getting thousands of rupees of royalty every month. When a new author asks them for information about the entire process, they neither answer nor provide any support, because their job is to discourage new authors and demoralize them. The path of deviating from the path of success and success starts from here. Whereas these authors who spread confusion are those whose only academic books have been published, they never tell the reality, they just keep watching the show silently by discouraging the new authors and breaking their morale. Obviously, the market of education is so big that children have to buy books, so here the author will also get royalty in thousands or lakhs.

It is also worth noting that sometimes authors who are senior in the world of literature and whose books are sold in their names also spread confusion. Obviously, when the author's name is enough to sell his books, then such an author does not need to spend for publishing, because the traditional publishers themselves offer such authors to publish their books. This topic has also been discussed in detail in the subsequent chapters.

Not only this, many times senior authors demoralize the new authors so much that the new authors stop even thinking about getting their book published. I have seen these authors misleading new authors even on the advertisements of self-publishers and saying, 'Oh! It is very sad that now publishers are taking money to publish books, whereas our books are published free of cost.' While they do not tell that this is an advertisement of a self-publishing company. Traditional publishers never advertise for self-publishing services. It is another matter that now traditional publishers have also entered the field of self-publishing.

Due to many such unwanted reasons and lack of information, many new passionate talented authors leave their talent and passion to rust by listening to people instead of listening to their heart. It can also be said that their passion cools down and they start feeling helpless. It seems to them that they do not have any such quality due to which they are not able to get any response from the publishers and the publishers do not want to publish their book. Whereas such authors, by denying reality, are themselves becoming obstacles in the way of their success.

Let me tell you that the reality is that traditional publishers do not publish your book very easily, because they always publish only well-known authors, so that publishers can get more chances to sell their book. Traditional publishers also publish books by well-known public sector philanthropists, social media celebrities, politicians and film artists because they do not have to spend much money on marketing their books.

Apart from the traditional publishing model, self-publishing model is also another available option, through which you can achieve success by publishing a book. About which many times the authors ignore it even after knowing, because the authors do not want to take risks. Due to which success passes them by despite their ability.

I have seen many authors getting frustrated who are talented and could go to any extent to promote their book, which is no less than a boon for them. Also, his writing is sharp and could have attracted the readers, but hearing from other people has ingrained the mentality of free publishing in his mind. Due to which such authors are never able to get their book published and their book remains limited to them only. Such authors often fail to become best-selling authors due to not listening to their heart.

The biggest thing is that if I don't believe in myself then why would anyone else believe in me. That means first you will have to take risks yourself, only then you will get new opportunities, otherwise you will not get any opportunities just by sitting back.

Always listen to your heart, because your success will be yours only, or your family's, rather your success will not be of the people who frustrate you. People who frustrate you will try to become close to you after your success, so that they can also achieve fame along with you.

The key to becoming a successful author is to not let the thinking of such people dominate you, which is stopping you from being successful. Always be in touch with or try to connect with successful authors or successful people who have made themselves successful through their own hard work. So that your mentality can be strengthened and you can establish new dimensions on the path of becoming a best seller author.

It is not that success is achieved just in a day or a year or a few years, success is achieved after falling again and again. But it is noteworthy that success achieved after repeated falls is permanent. At the same time, the success achieved with the help of others is momentary, which has no existence and such success is temporary. The decision is yours whether you want momentary success or permanent success.

If you are working hard on yourself as a author today and

listening to your heart, then no one can stop you from being among the successful authors. Those who are discouraging you will also want to join you in celebrating your success, because no one makes friends or even wants to have relations with unsuccessful people.

Remember that be it any business or struggle to become a successful author or any other work that can change your life or change your lifestyle, there will always be people ready to discourage you everywhere in your path. This has also been my own personal experience. When we do new work or take a risk, apart from society or acquaintances, many times even our family members do not support us. They discourage us, so that we deviate from our goals and live a life that will support our family or according to what they want. But keep in mind that to be successful we always have something to lose. Like, to become a successful author, you will have to devote your time to writing and after that you will have to invest time, money and heart for the success of the book.

Have you observed an ant carefully, it carries ten times its own weight, but never gives up. Apart from this, just see if a small bird can build its nest in one go. The answer is no, because the bird collects straws to make a nest and the bird has to make several trips to collect the straws, and then after many days of hard work the nest is ready.

Why can't we learn from these little creatures that success doesn't happen all at once? Why can't we take the message that continuous efforts are necessary to be successful? You read the biography of any successful author or businessman, they all fell many times, but even after falling they did not give up and today success lies at their feet.

It is very easy to become a author or poet, but becoming a successful author requires passion and continuous effort, for which only a few authors are able to make efforts and become successful authors.

That is, you may believe that to become a successful author you have to change your thinking and listen to your gut. If you just want to become a author then Amazon Kindle is available, upload the book there and it will be published.

Why are you wasting your time searching for any publisher? If you want to become a successful author, you will have to work for your success. Apart from this, you have to stop listening to people, because if you listen to people, then in the end you will not be able to get lost in the number of unsuccessful authors, because unsuccessful authors are those whom the readers read but did not like. After which he stopped writing or he could not muster the courage to write another book. Therefore, being an unsuccessful author is no less than a great achievement.

You can say that if you do not listen to your heart, you can become anonymous, because when you do not make efforts for success after listening to people, then no one will be able to read your book. So try, without the fear of failure, because behind every failure lies success.

become anonymous, because when you do not take self for or
success after flattering the people, then no one will be able to read
your book. So my. Without the fear of failure, because behind
every failure lies success.

Chapter 4

Write Something New for the Success of Your Book

Nowadays, due to the facility of social media and Facebook and WhatsApp, new poets and litterateurs are emerging in every small and big street and locality of every city of every state. The biggest thing to note is that everyone is proficient in the same genre or wants to be proficient in the same genre and want that my book should be published as soon as possible and become a best seller.

You have to understand very well that everyone is writing the same thing in the same genre in their own style, so who would want to read it again and again. I think you are reading this book of mine because perhaps its topic is completely different. Everyone often reads the books of many famous poets including Kumar Vishwas. Can you tell me how many books of poems written by new poets have you bought and read so far?

As far as my experience is concerned, you might have bought the books of your friends or relatives from the publisher on their request, but you would not have any interest in them. Many times you might have applauded or ignored their social media posts. I am not telling you wrong, but this is nothing new, because because of your friendship or closeness with the author, one has to praise them. But due to such praise, new authors or poets often fall into the misconception that once their book is published, no one can stop them from becoming a best-selling author.

Apart from this, you have many friends or acquaintances who show beautiful dreams to the author and say wow! Brother or sister, you write very beautiful poetry, no one can write better than you, only you can become the next best seller author, why don't you get the book published. We will remain the first readers.

After reading many such comments, when the author gets

excited and self-publishes his book, the fans giving advice are not visible even when seen through a powerful telescope like the Hubble Telescope. After all this, the book fails and the author starts finding fault with the self-publisher's work. The publisher did not work for the marketing of my book, the publisher did not do the promotion and all of them are running the publishing house to make money. It is 100 percent true that self-publishing houses are being run only to earn profits, which is providing employment to many people. This has been discussed in detail in the subsequent pages of the book.

I would like to advise new authors that you should not just sheepishly write what everyone else is writing. You write that which is new for everyone, which everyone wants to read. Always study new topics, buy and read books on new topics, write on new topics and try to connect with your potential readers.

Apart from this, go to the local bookstores of your city and buy new best seller books and ask the shopkeeper what people are liking to read, or on which subject books are being bought the most.

Apart from this task, ask or get information from your friends or colleagues or other relatives about their interests. Go to any library in your city, read the most read books there and observe what their authors have written. So that you can get a topic for your future book.

Always keep in mind that whatever you are writing, write it only for one readership among whom you want to reach your book. For example, when Chetan Bhagat writes for the youth, the young readers like his books very much. There are many other authors who have their own readership, and they write as per their choice, because one of the keys to success is that we have to set our goals.

Nowadays the trend is that if one author is writing a poem, the other author will also write poetry. Everyone's effort is to write the best poem, and there is a flood of applause on social media. Many times, in the misunderstanding of this praise, some poets also get these poems self-published in the form of a book, but the result is the same, which I had mentioned on the previous pages of this book. That means, the result is zero.

If writing is your hobby then maintain it and do research on new topics, because success is achieved by falling again and again or by continuous efforts. If success is achieved once, there will be abundance of successful people all over the world. Then where will the unsuccessful people go, and why will the successful people be discussed? Or why would successful people be considered as our role models?

Hence, it is obvious that to climb the ladder of success you will have to work hard. Not only hard work, you will have to do market research and apart from this, you will also have to read continuously. Know this well that you cannot write better unless you read other authors. So read more and write less. Write only that which can take you towards success. Think something new and write something new. You will definitely get success, but always by trying something new.

If you are writing just for hobby then it is good, keep writing, but do not think about success. If you are writing for success then write for success, because there is a lot of difference between writing for hobby and writing for success. In my knowledge, there are many authors who believe that it does not matter to them whether their books are sold or not, hence they always look for the cheapest way to publish their books, because they just want to fulfill their hobby.

While there are some authors who are writing for success, but what they write cannot make them successful because no one wants to read what they are writing. It is noteworthy that readers want to read what is new to them. Amish Tripathi wrote the story of Indian culture and mythology in a new style, which was immediately accepted by the readers. Today Amish's books have been published in many languages around the world, for which he is continuously receiving royalties worth lakhs of rupees.

It is also noteworthy that a Hollywood film has also been made on the story written by Amish Tripathi. An American producer has offered a very good deal for the story rights of the author of 'The Immortals of Meluhha', 'The Secret of Nagas' and 'The Oath of the Vayuputraja'.

Amish has achieved success because of his hard work, continuous efforts and writing something new. If he had not worked hard or had given up after failing in his first attempt, he might never have got such big offers. Neither you or I would have known them and they would have been living an ordinary life.

Chapter 5

Don't waste Time Dreaming of Traditional Publishing

Being in the publishing industry, according to my experience, at present every writer or poet wants that his book gets published under the traditional model and becomes a best seller. Whereas the reality is that traditional publishers always publish books of such authors who have already established their good identity among the readers or among the public on their own or their actual fan following counts in millions. So that the pre-booking of books in the name of an established author can be done in thousands or even lakhs. Traditional publishers never bet on new authors, they always bet on already established authors like race horses in a race course.

Think, why don't traditional publishers publish only established authors? The simple thing is that traditional publishers print only 50-100 copies, they print lakhs of copies and they have to sell the books under the name of the author.

Secondly, the name of the publisher itself is no less important, because many generations of hard work and continuous investment have been made to take the publication to the heights. Due to which they do not publish new authors, so that they can also get their business benefits.

In such a situation, the publisher has to keep in mind that he has to pay royalty to the author and also cover the expenses of promotion of the book. They also have to save for the future of their company, save from profits for their staff and daily office expenses. Otherwise, if any traditional publisher does not think from a business perspective, after publishing a book, he will have to go bankrupt and stop publishing, which will lead to loss of many jobs.

In my journey so far in the publishing industry, I have seen many publications opening and closing, which started but closed because they could not understand the authors. Some did not understand the publishing industry and due to providing free publishing facilities as per the wishes of the authors, they were not able to pay the salaries of the staff and meet the office expenses. Due to which the publishing houses themselves were closed. At the same time, some publishers could not adapt to technology with time, due to which their publishing houses died.

Do you know that the closure of a publishing house does not only cause loss to the publisher, it also causes loss to the authors and employees who were associated with them, because the author's book would at least be available on the online store, so that the author can Its identity would remain intact and it would get some royalty if sold. Apart from this, employees also had to turn to new institutions for their livelihood. That is, the publishing industry is also a universal business model, and not a social service organization. But it is also noteworthy that if social service organizations do not get financial support from anywhere, they will also close down, because they too do not have enough money to keep their organization going through their own expenses. Whereas publishers do not get any external financial support.

As it has been my experience, at present every new author, after writing one or two articles or poems or stories, wants the traditional publisher to make such a huge investment on his book, which in some way is detrimental to the publisher's economy. It is not possible and no publisher will do so, because without the economy no one can save the publisher from bankruptcy.

If you too are harboring the dream of getting published by a traditional publisher, then you should give up the dream of becoming a successful or best-selling author. For such authors who cannot take risks for themselves, even God himself cannot come on earth and do anything for them. To become a successful author, it is necessary for the author to work on the ground himself. Only then can the author achieve success and enjoy success. Becoming a successful author means that, impressed by your success, the traditional publisher itself offers you to publish your new book.

I often talk to authors and try to understand them. But the mindset of most authors is that they neither have to work hard nor have any expenses. Only if his book gets published. The biggest thing is that when you are well aware that the self-publishing company charges for publishing the book, then why are you wasting your time going to them. Yet authors constantly register themselves on the ads of self-publishing companies and request to publish a book for free. While this is just wasting the author's time, if the author spends this time on the content and marketing of his book, then perhaps he can get success.

A few days ago, I got a call from a author who said that we should give you money as well as our content. This is not justice to a author. My simple answer to him was that we neither want your content nor your money. If you think that you can get the book published by paying money then you are wholeheartedly welcome, otherwise we cannot help you. The second thing is that we have not come to you with an offer, you yourself have come to us, because if you have a need, then you yourself decide for it. After this, his reply was that you can buy our book, don't pay us royalty, you will keep the copyright as well, just give us a lump sum amount.

Then I replied to him that sir, our publishing house does not want your content, because we are a self-publishing company and we provide publishing services to the author for a fee. What will we do by taking the copyright of your book, where will we sell it, because no one knows you. Now you will say that you will publish, only then anyone will know the author. But you think and tell why someone should publish such authors, which causes financial loss to the publisher and the author does not want to bear the expenses of publishing, marketing or promoting the book on his own behalf.

This is not the story of just one author, many such authors call and e-mail throughout the day. If free services are provided to everyone then I can say with certainty that the publishing house will go bankrupt, because if the author himself does not put in some hard work then there is no guarantee of the success of his book. Those authors who want to play the next innings by placing the gun on the publisher's shoulder. Such authors are not successful in life.

Now you must have understood how authors often try just to get published and not to become best-selling authors. Often authors waste their time in this way by going to self-publishing publishers, whereas they do not get any benefit from it, because the self-publishing company does not provide you free publishing services. You should try going to a traditional publisher and giving them information about your book. Also assure them that your book will become a best seller. If you yourself believe in the success of your book, then definitely try once.

Think for yourself, if you have your own readership or you have your own branding as an author then why would any traditional publisher refuse to publish your book. It may be possible that traditional publishers themselves may be impressed by your branding and make an offer for you. Even if traditional publishers don't make you an offer if you approach them directly, they won't be able to turn you down because you've worked hard to brand yourself as a author. You have your own readership and your own fan following.

If you think that you will be able to sell your book on the basis of your strong personality or your book will be sold only by your name. Then my advice is to contact your preferred traditional publisher, convince them that your name or face is enough to get your book sold. If even after these efforts you do not get a deal with a traditional publisher, you can also contact a self-publishing publisher. Make an agreement in writing with the self-publisher that more than a thousand copies will be sold in your name, if not sold, you will bear the expenses incurred on their time and printing of the book. Also, discuss openly the percentage of royalty and ask for the percentage of royalty in writing from the publisher. But do not try this trick on my publishing house, because my experience in this matter has been very bad, I have published for free many such authors who had made similar empty claims.

According to the belief that has settled in the minds of authors, pressure was put on me by many authors regarding the right to publish free of cost. Initially my publishing house published books of many authors free of cost, but during this time I realized that free publication or facility has no importance. Apart from this, not only I, no person in the world can fulfill the wishes of all the authors or all the wishes of the world even by sacrificing everything. After being published free of cost, due to lack of support from the authors, the books published by me were hardly sold and the authors also never made any effort. Due to which I continued to suffer financial losses. Due to many such problems, I had become mentally unwell. In such bad circumstances, I started regretting that I had spent my precious time and money on the wrong business model.

Ultimately, due to continuous financial losses, my publishing house went bankrupt and the publishing house remained closed for about one and a half years. But due to my habit of reading books, I was reading motivational books even in those days, which inspired me to start a new innings again. Before starting a new innings, I studied and researched very thoroughly about self-publishing and traditional publishing models, so that I can come back stronger than before, because the world makes fun of you after your failure.

Apart from this, after continuously studying many motivational books, I also understood that success is never achieved by running away from the fear of failure and by listening to the people of the society, Lack of knowledge about your business or goal and changing one's decisions again and again. I also understood that even if one puts everything at stake to do what the authors want, even ignoring the aspirations of one's family, the authors' aspirations cannot be fulfilled, because you can never Cannot fulfill the aspirations of everyone in the world. Despite every effort you make, one or the other deficiency definitely remains. Apart from this, you should do whatever is best for you and the livelihood of the employees working in your office. Don't do what the world wants. Always do your work honestly and always be honest towards your customers in your business. This was my own personal experience, now coming to the main topic.

If you feel that you will not be able to sell your book under your own name, then give up the idea of getting your book published traditionally or consider spending money and getting the book published under the self-publishing model. If you really want to become a successful author. It is another matter that if you do not want to get the book published even for a fee, then give up the idea of publishing the book, because you have no passion to become a successful author. You just have to get the book published, not be successful.

I would like to tell you that at present many so-called traditional publishers are also providing their services, who are giving authors the opportunity to get published traditionally by printing fifty to hundred copies. These publishers may just fulfill your dream of getting published, but always keep in mind that success cannot be achieved just by doing so.

It is also worth noting here that such so-called traditional publishers are unable to bring the author's book among the readers on a large scale like an established traditional publisher. They lack the resources and large-scale marketing strategies to deliver books to a large audience, as well as the ability to invest in their publishing house or the author's book. Also, such publishers do not do any work on the quality of the manuscript, marketing and branding of the book, they just publish the author's book and try to sell the book through the author's reader circle. In the end, the author's book is forgotten after making it available on the online platform. That is, whoever needs it or wants to read it will buy it and read it, because many times such so-called traditional publishers print only twenty to thirty copies. If they realize that the demand for copies is increasing then they print more copies, otherwise after some time the author's books start appearing out of stock on the online platform.

Many times these traditional publishers also have a condition that they will not pay any royalty to the author until 100 copies are sold. Apart from this, it is also worth noting that most of the traditional publishers operating on a small scale cover their printing expenses by forcing the author to buy the author's copies. In some cases publishing terms include a requirement for the author to purchase the book before or after publication. That is, even for the so-called traditional publishers, the first priority is to cover the printing and designing expenses, because they too have to maintain the existence of their publication.

Now ask yourself, are you ready to become a successful author? Consider through which medium you want to get your book published and start making efforts to become a successful author.

Chapter 6

Work on Building Yourself An Impressive Brand

Whether you have published your book under the self-publishing model or the traditional publishing model. If you have not made any efforts to promote your book, then it is also possible that you are not serious about the success of your book.

You must have often noticed that whenever a new film is

launched, its stars inspire people to watch their film. Film stars go from one city to another to promote their film, so that their film attracts more audiences and their film gets more profits. Whereas many stars know that most of the profits will go into the pockets of their production company. But despite knowing everything, their aim is to promote themselves through films, because if their film becomes a hit, then their chances of getting work from other filmmakers will increase a lot. If the film flops then other film producers will also distance themselves from them and will not give them the opportunity to work in their films, because every person or organization in this world wants to work only with successful people.

The author also has to understand that if his first book is successful then you will not have to work hard to publish your next book, because you have already worked hard to create your readership. Secondly, given your large readership and the success of your book, traditional publishers may consider going ahead with publishing you.

Now you will say that if the artist gets good money in the film, then why does the author not get it? While the author is also working hard. I am well aware that this question might have come to most people's mind, but I have the answer. Tell me, are the actors of big or small budget films new? All the viewers know that no filmmaker wants to invest in a new artist, because they do not trust the new artist. Every filmmaker wants to invest money on an already established artist, because he knows that he has crores of fans, due to which his film will not suffer financial loss. If he bets on a new artist then the chances of success of his film are negligible.

It is also well known that many film producers have given opportunities to new artists, but the films of those artists who have worked hard on their own promotion have also been successful and they have been getting work continuously.

At the same time, many artists did not make any effort to promote their films by taking fees, due to which their films failed and they stopped getting work. Such artists are living an anonymous life today.

Simply, this is the business strategy of the traditional publisher as well, he also does not want to invest in a new author. Until authors establish themselves, they tend to bet on older established authors because they know they will get their investment back with profits.

If you really want to make a career as a successful author then you have to work like a combative and hardworking person. Who focuses only on his goal, who pays less attention to money and focuses on his future. You will have to work like a young leader who dedicates half his life to politics and gets results after many years of penance.

Many times young leaders know that it is not necessary that they will get the results of their hard work. But despite knowing all this, a leader puts everything at stake for his political career, even his personal career. Even after all this, he does not stop struggling, only then he achieves his desired position in politics. Many times, this success comes at the last stage of life, but they do not complain about it, because they know that they have got the results of their hard work.

Chapter 7

Don't Waste Your Precious Time Chasing High Royalty

In Shrimad Bhagwat Geeta, Shri Krishna says to Arjun that hey! Parth, you do the work, it is my job to give results. But ignoring this statement, most authors desire higher royalties along with looking for a cheaper publisher. While they do not think about making their book successful through a cheap publisher or they do not take into account the opportunity to establish or prove themselves through a cheap publisher. They just want more profits.

It is noteworthy that if you invest in your today, your tomorrow can be golden. That is to say, instead of earning profits in the present, you should prepare a blue print to earn bigger profits in the future. Always remember, success can be decided or the future can be secured only through your own foresight.

I often hear from authors that my book is ready for publication, but they are unable to reach an agreement with any publisher regarding royalties. I am not getting the royalties as per my expectation. Self publishing company is not giving me royalty and facilities as per my demand. Whereas such authors want a lot of facilities and high royalty along with nominal expenses for publishing their book. Whereas such authors do not set their goals. They just want facilities and high royalties. Due to which success keeps going away from them and in the end goes very far away.

Whereas if the authors focus their aim only on establishing their own identity, then in future they will not need to wander for profit. I have read about many authors who were not known to anyone, but who worked hard to establish their identity in the early stages of their writing careers and continued to struggle, ignoring the lure of higher royalties. He did not aim for more royalties or profits and simply strived for success. His goal was to earn more profit in the future, not to earn profit in his initial journey.

Those authors today charge lakhs of rupees for speaking on stage for ten minutes or appearing in any program, because they have worked hard for their own success. It is also noteworthy that the organizers consider it an honor to invite them by paying lakhs of rupees. This is the result of those authors' own hard work and not succumbing to raw greed.

It is true that if we start thinking about big benefits before starting any work then it is impossible to achieve success. Look at the example of Reliance Jio, if it had not given free data in the beginning and started thinking about its profits from the very beginning, then perhaps it would not have been in the profitable position it is in today. It would also have been providing its services like other telecom companies and there would have been many options available in the telecom market, due to which the number of its customers would not have been as much as it is at present.

Reliance Jio thought about future profits and did not make any efforts to earn profits in the beginning itself. Due to which he is in a profitable position today. Similarly, for example, you will get the biographies of many authors to read in Google search, which give us the message that to be successful, our focus should be towards the goal and not towards profit or result. To be successful, we should focus only on the goal and not on the profit or result.

I want to explain to you that if you really want to make money from your book then never chase high royalties. Instead, work on your own branding to attract royalty by becoming a successful author.

It is noteworthy that money works like a magnet, which can be attracted only by success. Let us tell you that many world class famous motivational authors and speakers have also written this statement in their books. He has emphasized more that success comes through continuous efforts and focus on the goal.

Suppose you finalize a deal with a self-publishing publisher on higher royalties, how many books will you be able to sell, hardly a maximum of fifty copies. Whereas this number is also very high, because new authors have to face a lot of problems to sell their books. How much money did you make from these fifty copies? As far as my experience says, even your self-publishing charges will not be recovered. If you just publish the book and work on marketing your book, then it is possible that due to your hard work you will be able to sell thousands of books and along with recovering the self-publishing charges, you will also get the key to your success. If thousands of copies are sold then understand that you have climbed a few steps in the list of successful authors.

If you sell thousands of copies, then it is obvious that you can go to any traditional publisher and propose to publish your new book. You can tell him that I have sold thousands of copies and I have my own readership, so I want the royalty percentage as per my wish. It is obvious that everyone wants to work with successful people, so in such a situation it is possible that the publisher may consider publishing your book.

Always keep this in mind that due to the greed for more royalty, you will be able to earn only a few rupees by selling a few books, whereas if you struggle for the success of the book, you will not have to struggle for the royalty. Always keep in mind that after achieving success, you can earn money through many means, because for a successful person, many paths to earn money automatically open up. Many times many big brands themselves invite them to work with them. Now it is up to you to decide whether a few royalties are important to you in the present time, or whether being successful in the future and earning more profits is more important to you.

Chapter 8

Maintain Confidence and do not Let Your Morale Fall

If you want to become a successful author then never be afraid of struggle and never give up. Keep working hard and struggling continuously, because success is not achieved in a day or a night. Success is achieved after many years of hard work and patience, so always maintain your confidence and do not let your morale fall. It is also worth noting that success achieved through shortcuts does not last long. Hard work, consistent effort, and a long time are all very important factors for lasting success.

One of the main reasons why many authors fail is lack of confidence in their writing ability. Many authors struggle with self-doubt and fear, which can make it challenging for them to take the risks necessary to succeed as a author. In such a situation, authors often lose self-confidence, due to which they go astray or try to prove themselves right by pointing out the shortcomings of others. In such circumstances they are not able to succeed.

Another reason many authors fail is their lack of perseverance and patience. I can understand that writing can be a long and difficult process. If an author takes a long time to write his book, but faces rejection from a traditional publisher, he gets discouraged. To overcome this, you have to constantly strive for success and remind yourself that success as a author often requires time and patience.

Moreover, another reason behind the failure of many authors is the lack of knowledge about the publishing industry and the interest of the readers. Many authors fail because they do not know much about the publishing industry and at times they do not understand the interests of the readers for whom they are writing.

Many times authors keep writing without paying attention to the readership and due to which they are not able to select the right readership. In such a situation, they select a wrong readership and try unsuccessfully to sell their book among them, due to which they face failure.

Many times authors do not want to learn and do not want to do anything new, they consider what they are writing or what they like as the best and want to be successful only on the basis of that. Which is wrong, a author should learn and try to write content that readers want to read. Only then can the author become the favorite author of the readers.

There are many authors who expect overnight success and want a publisher to give them an opportunity to publish and make them a best seller overnight. Which is not only possible but impossible without the hard work of the author.

I have experienced that often authors want to earn too much royalty from their writing. While they don't want to work on their writing or their skills. Many times they think they are better, they don't need to learn or sharpen their skills.

Who doesn't want to get money and fame, but many authors dream of becoming authors for money and fame. But they want to achieve it easily, which is not possible for them. To achieve money and fame they need to make continuous efforts and efforts.

There are many authors who somehow want to become famous authors by selling millions of copies overnight, which is not possible, because success is achieved over many years of hard work and consistent efforts.

Always keep in mind that inspiration is always needed to become a successful author. If you are writing just for money, you will not be able to achieve success through your writing, because your focus is just on money. Due to which you deviate from the path of continuous efforts and improving the quality of your writing skills.

If you search successful authors on Google, you will find many such authors who remained adamant on their passion for writing and kept writing to fulfill their desire and such authors have also become famous. Who are also earning good money today, because they just focused on writing and skills. If he had concentrated on earning money in the form of royalty in the beginning, perhaps he would not have been successful today.

Unsuccessful authors often write and sometimes write a book as quickly as possible, but then stop. Don't like to carefully revise or edit your book and don't even try to get your book published through self-publishing. Due to which he remains an unsuccessful author throughout his life. I have edited this book more than ten times and every time I found mistakes in it. Which I corrected and also sent the PDF to some close authors for reading.

There are very few successful authors who have written only one book. To become a successful author, you will have to keep writing continuously, keep publishing books continuously, and apart from this, you will have to continuously work on new strategies for promotion.

Often many authors accept some lies related to success as true, some of which are as follows-

1. The biggest popular lie is that publishing any author's book for free is the mark of the author's success. Which is the mentality of most authors, due to which they are not able to make efforts for their success throughout their life.

2. Publishers are preventing authors from being successful by not giving them the opportunity of free publication. It is another matter that apart from traditional publishers, authors also expect free services from self-publishers. Which is not possible according to the self-publishing business model.

3. I am poor or my financial condition is not good, therefore I cannot succeed or have not been able to succeed. Whereas it is worth noting that no better efforts are made from the author's side.

4. I am too young or too old to be a successful author. Whereas there is no age restriction for success.

5. My luck is bad or my publisher (self publishing company) did not do anything for the promotion and marketing of my book or I am not destined to become a best seller author or it is not written in my destiny to become a author, hence I

Couldn't get success in writing.

Self-publishing and traditional publishing are explained in detail in the next pages of the book, which need to be read carefully.

Apart from this, there are many other things due to which authors become afraid or lose courage in setting their goals, but all these things are completely false. The truth is that you can achieve what you want with your hard work and struggle. To achieve it you just need to have passion and the intention to never give up. If you have passion and the will to win, then no force can stop you from becoming a successful author.

There are some authors who find a self-publishing company as per their need or budget. But now in such a situation the demand for such authors increases a lot. Like their book should also be available in book fairs, they should get more royalty, their book should also be available in the offline market. Whereas it is worth noting that self-publishers provide all these facilities to authors with a budget of at least lakhs of rupees.

Due to many such demands, the self publishing company tells them the charges, and due to high charges, in the end the author is not ready for publication and he starts finding shortcomings of the self publisher. Whereas such authors are never serious about their success and goals.

Such authors just want to achieve success with lots of features at low fees, because if the book is available offline, there will be a possibility of selling it in large numbers. Even if the book goes to a book fair, there will be a possibility of reaching thousands of readers and there are many such things which the author imagines. Whereas they shy away from taking risks. Always keep in mind that only the author who can take risks can achieve success.

It is worth noting here that no self-publisher can give you success even by charging high fees, because for success you will have to work hard. I have seen advertisements from some publishers who guarantee authors to become best sellers and money back if they do not become best sellers. But it is worth noting that such publishers tell the author a separate marketing budget of at least lakhs of rupees. Whereas let me tell you that if you do not become a best seller author, only the money that you have paid for self-publishing is refunded to you. That is, only the fee for the self-publishing package will be refunded, not the promotion fee worth lakhs. Thus, without hard work or a solid marketing plan, no self-publisher or traditional publisher can ever turn an author into a best-selling author.

Chapter 9

Learn from the Experiences of Successful Self-published Authors

No one ever achieves success by giving up. You can get inspiration for success from self-published authors who never gave up. This chapter covers some of the prominent and famous self-published authors who have achieved success by self-publishing their books. I am sure you will be inspired by reading about these authors.

If your book has been rejected by a traditional publisher and you are disappointed, you must read this comment by Ashwin Sanghi, one of India's most read authors, in his own words. He said 'I am probably the most rejected author in the world. I was rejected 47 times by both traditional publishing houses and literary agents.

In an interview given to Your Story.com website, Ashwin Sanghi said that no author gets success overnight and in today's time, it is important to be patient and take advantage of technology in publishing.

In an interview given to Your Story.com website, he said that 'the self-publishing model did not exist before 2007. In fact, the only facility that existed in those days was the vanity press. Through which in those days you could get copies of your book printed.

Sanghi says, 'My experience as a self-published author taught me the intricacies of marketing and promoting a book. When you are a self-published author, you are like the CEO, marketing director, production in-charge and manager of your book, meaning you are doing everything.'

Amish Tripathi, the banker whose manuscript was rejected by about 20 traditional publishers. Amish Tripathi self-published his first book "The Immortals of Meluha" after his manuscript was rejected and has become India's fastest selling author. More than 1.7 million copies of his books have been sold, generating an amount of Rs 40 crore. Additionally he received an unprecedented amount of Rs 5 crore as advance for his next series.

Best-selling author Savi Sharma told in an interview to a website FinancialExpress.com that she had self-published her first book. I started promoting my book on Facebook. I shared many inspirational quotes from my book on social media in the form of posters. Through such social media posts and advertisements, 5,000 copies of my book were sold in a month. After the success of my book, I started getting calls from traditional publishing houses to republish my book with them.

Savi Sharma says that people often say that self-publishing is a bad option, because you cannot sell more books through it. She says that if you know how to go through the whole process, you can sell your book yourself, this is a great opportunity today. But, apart from this you need to learn many things, one of which is how to connect with readers. If you do this effectively, you can succeed.

Young novelist Durjoy Dutta says in an interview to India Today, 'I still keep reading a lot, because when you read, you are constantly learning new things about writing a story, and You may discover new things you want to include in your writing.

He said that every author, whether established or not, has to face struggles.

Apart from these authors, you can also read about other famous self-authors, including Ashish Bagrecha, Anubhav Aggarwal, Rupi Kaur, Devika Das, Rashmi Trivedi, Arun Bhatnagar, Shubham Shukla. All these authors are self-published authors, who have achieved success after their hard work and continuous efforts.

Let me tell you that this author is not only a author of good stories but he has also successfully self-published his books despite many difficulties. You too can be inspired by their experiences for self-publishing. If you want to be successful in life as a author then it can be a good option for you to learn and get inspiration from the experiences of self-published authors. There are many self-published authors in India too, who self-published their books and achieved success.

Well-known self-published authors write books according to the interests of readers and dedicate themselves to promoting their book. Many times these famous authors continue to move ahead on the path of struggle with patience while facing difficulties. Such authors continue their efforts to achieve their goals and read motivational books to keep their spirits high.

Furthermore, self-published authors must be in direct contact with their readers, which helps them understand the readers' interests. Successful self-published authors always understand their target market or readers well and write their books keeping in mind the interests of that market or readers. If you read the biography of any successful self-published author, you will know that such authors work actively to promote their books and learn from past experiences to make new plans for the next book or promotion plan.

Note: In this article, about famous self-published authors, the statements spoken by them and data related to their books, from interviews and articles published on various websites, the author of the book 'How to become a best-selling author' has written in his own words, Therefore, the author of the book 'How to Become a Best Seller Author' does not vouch for the authenticity of any details in this article related to famous self-published authors and their book sales figures or actual earnings.

Chapter 10

Successful Authors Never Copy Others

To achieve success, this is also a formula to never copy others. Always do new experiments with your writing, write something new, so that your writing can hold the edge of success.

If you think that an author had written a book which became successful and I should also write on it, then you are wrong. You should try to write something new from your level. You write what has not been written yet. You can write on topics or issues that can make you go viral overnight.

Also keep in mind that going viral overnight does not mean that you will immediately become a best-selling author, or earn millions in royalties from day one. If you read the books of big successful authors, you will realize that they never copy other authors, because they have their own writing style.

Successful authors create their own stories, they do research for their stories, read books, and create characters for their stories. Successful authors take many years to complete their book. If you also want to become a successful author then give time to writing your book. Research the topic you are writing on.

No one can know better than you what you write or what you want to write. It is also worth noting that always select your favorite subject, but there should be some newness in it. Today's reader wants something new and readers also want to read new authors, provided there is something new in the new author's book.

Never copy others to be successful, if you think that Kumar Vishwas just writes poems that is why he has become famous. You would think that if I also write poems then readers will like my book also. The answer to this is not at all, because Kumar Vishwas did not suddenly become popular among the readers, he recited poems on the stage, but keeping the youth in mind. His poems had something new and the way he presented his poetry impressed the mind of every reader. As is his poem - Koi Diwana Kahta Hai, To Koi Pagal Samajhta Hai.

If you want to write a story of success, then write something that hits the reader's tongue, or say that the reader keeps humming it or discusses it everywhere. Because if your poem or story is discussed then the demand will increase and if the demand increases then you will get success. There are many authors who have written many such books which became successful overnight. Due to which those authors have become successful authors today.

If you also think that if you write on the topic selected by them, your book will also become successful, then you are going in the wrong direction. You will have to write something different from their topic. What this means is that you should not write by copying other authors. Keep thinking, keep reading new and old books, so that you can get new ideas for your book.

Chapter 11

Plan for Marketing and Promotion of Your Book

I have often noticed that most of the authors are not aware about the marketing and promotion of their book after self-publishing. Due to which his book does not find readers. For the success of your book, you will also have to pay attention to marketing and promotion, which will determine the success of your book. If you ignore this then you are not doing justice to the success of your book. Currently, there are many social media websites on the internet, which do not charge any fee. You can take advantage of these websites for the promotion of your book.

There are many successful authors who have made their book a best seller through social media websites. Best-selling authors including Ashish Bagrecha, Rupi Kaur and Savi Sharma inspired readers to read their books through Instagram and other social media websites. Today all these names are included in the count of successful authors. Like these successful authors, you can also use social media websites to promote your book, but you will also have to work continuously. Many times authors post for a few days and after that they find this work monotonous, due to which they are deprived of success.

Before promoting on social media, first of all you have to select the readership for your book. That is, you must first clarify the goal of your book and you will have to decide among which readership you want to promote your book and what age group of readers will be your target.

Also, you can create your own blog or website and share updates on it from time to time, because if readers get to read your posts from time to time, they can become fans of your writing. You can publish your readers' reviews along with their photos on your website or blog. Impressed by this, your readers will share the link of your blog in their circle and the chances of increasing your readership can increase manifold.

Apart from social media, you can also promote your book offline through friends, family and colleagues. Also buy and read best seller books related to marketing and promotion, because best seller marketing books will teach you a lot of marketing tips and will also inspire you to do some new experiments. Many times we are unable to think outside our circle. In such a situation, if we read such books which inspire us or inspire us to do some new experiments. You can also search for articles and tips related to book marketing or promotion on Google. Along with this, many other tools and websites are available on the internet for book promotion, learn to use them. There are many websites that publish author interviews and book reviews, giving the author an opportunity to be highlighted.

If you have a budget for the promotion of your book, you can take the services of an experienced marketing agency. Which will work keeping in mind the intended readers of your book. Regarding promotion, I would like to say that as creative as you can be, this can be a better option for promoting your book. Because no one else can do the promotion for your book or for yourself as wholeheartedly as you can. I would advise you that you must make a marketing and promotion plan for your success, because what is visible sells and what is not visible does not sell.

Therefore, your effort should be to promote your book as much as possible. So that the path to your success can be paved. Some promotion tips are given in the subsequent chapters of the book, which will prove beneficial for you.

Chapter 12

Difference between Self Publishing and Traditional Publishing Model

Being in the publishing business, I come across many authors every day, most of them just requesting for free book publishing service. Some authors object to the fact that why are publishers taking money for publishing books?

As I have mentioned on the previous pages of the book, there is a misconception among authors that the author has the right to publish his book for free. As far as I have read many books in this regard and articles on many websites found through Google search. Even to my knowledge, there is no fundamental right of the authors in which there is mention of publishing the author's book for free. But for your information, let me tell you that book publishing mainly works on two types of models – Traditional Publishing and Self Publishing, that is, there are two types of publishers. Out of which one is a traditional publisher and the other is a self-publisher. If you are a author then it is important for you to know the difference between the two types of publishers.

Traditional publishing model

Traditional publishers publish the author's books completely free of cost, such publishers are called traditional publishers. But this does not at all mean that every author's books are guaranteed to be published. Yes, you are reading it right, traditional publishers often decide to publish an author's book for free (traditionally) only after observing the author's strong profile, content and the author's own readership or followers.

Sometimes, according to the high profile of the author, advance payment is also made in the form of royalty. If the publisher feels that the author's profile or followers or the author's content is not strong, they reject the author's proposal or manuscript without giving any reason.

At the same time, if your manuscript is accepted by a traditional publisher, then it is a great opportunity for you. After your manuscript is accepted by a traditional publisher, it can take at least six months to a few years to get from the publishing process to the market. After the book is published, royalty is paid to the author on an annual basis.

It is worth noting that often in the traditional publishing model, the publisher's team takes decisions for all important tasks including book cover to marketing strategy. That means the publisher's decision is the final decision, no advice or suggestions are taken from the author. You can understand that the author is limited to just handing over his manuscript to the publisher.

It is also worth noting that if your social profile is very strong and your own actual fan following is very high or your name is enough to sell books, then in such a situation you should approach a traditional publisher only. I am giving this advice because traditional publishers give more importance to such authors. The publisher expects from such authors that their costs and expenses will be covered and they will also earn profits. It is obvious that if the publisher earns profit then the royalty of the author will also be decent.

It is also a bitter truth in the traditional publishing model that traditional publishers want to publish already famous authors because it is a profitable deal for them. As far as new authors are concerned, traditional publishers prefer to publish well-known names or those who have already made a big name for themselves in their respective fields. Such as famous film stars, television personalities, sportspersons, politicians, social media stars, fashion models, celebrities and youth icons because the first book written by a celebrity has very high chances of sales. So if you want to get your first book published by a big traditional publisher, you have to first become famous in some field, and then approach the traditional publisher.

Traditional publishers are never interested in new authors, even if their content is strong, because there is a lot of expense and hard work involved in promoting and distributing their first book. At the same time, they know that even the books of new authors do not sell more than a few hundred copies. Traditional publishers always want to publish books that can earn maximum profit with minimum effort.

If you are a new author and send some sample manuscripts of your first book to well-known traditional publishers for review, there is a 100% chance that you will not get any response. But some of those traditional publishers may be so practical that they may return your sample manuscript with a predetermined rejection format, which may clearly state that your book is not possible to publish.

Many authors have said in their experiences that many times the author's manuscript is returned by traditional publishers without being read or opened.

Benefits of traditional publishing

The biggest advantage of traditional publishing is that the author does not need to spend even a single rupee to publish his book. The author has to submit his manuscript to the publisher. The rest of the work is done by the publisher's experienced team. Editing, layout, proof reading, printing and marketing of the author's book are all done by the publisher's experienced team.

The good thing about the traditional publishing business model is that traditional publishers have a large sales network with various bookstores, libraries, online retailers and other sales points, which ensures wide distribution of the author's books.

Due to the extended distribution network of traditional publishers, thousands to millions of copies of the author's book are guaranteed to be sold. Due to which the author's book has greater chances of success and getting more royalty benefits. Apart from this, since the traditional publisher has an experienced marketing team, promotion team and an extended national and international distribution network, there is no doubt about the success of the book.

If your book is published through a traditional publisher,

your chances of getting offers for book publishing from other publishers increase significantly, because your books and your name have established their dominance in the market.

Disadvantages of traditional publishing

Many traditional publishers do not accept manuscripts directly from authors, preferring to go through established literary agents. Due to which the new author has to pay fees to literary agents. While it is worth noting that after paying literary agents, your book is guaranteed to be published, but yes, the chances of getting the book published are higher because the literary agent goes ahead only after reviewing your manuscript. The literary agent system is not very popular in India, but a similar role is sometimes played by established authors in India, whose job is to act as a bridge between new authors and the traditional publisher.

Many times such established authors break the morale of new authors coming into the writing field and do not encourage them. Many times such literary agents take payment from authors and mislead them that their manuscript has been rejected. Due to which authors suffer financial loss and their morale also falls. This has happened with some authors I know, they told me that their manuscripts were published by so-called literary agents in their own name and some manuscripts were published in someone else's name. Which is a very sad incident for any author.

I would advise authors to always approach a traditional

publisher directly and not through any literary agent. So that your manuscript and your hard work cannot be misused.

Another downside of traditional publishing is that once the author signs the contract and hands over the manuscript to the publisher, his involvement in the entire process of editing, proof-reading and designing the book remains negligible. In traditional publishing, the author does not even have the right to determine the maximum selling price of his book.

Any kind of amendments or changes can be made to the author's manuscript by the traditional publisher, which the author has to accept in any case. If the author does not accept changes to his manuscript, the chance that his manuscript will be rejected is as high as 99.99%.

Additionally, in the traditional publishing model all communication is done via email, you are never contacted over a phone call. Nor can you call again and again to know the progress report of your book, because no updates are given to you regarding the publishing progress of your book. You are given updates only after your book is published.

In most traditional publishers' contracts, all the terms and conditions are in favor of the publisher. Note that often new authors sign book publishing contracts without much knowledge or thinking about them, because they are getting the benefit of publishing the book from a traditional publisher. Which is no less than a dream for them. Contracts with traditional publishers often include exclusive rights to print and distribute the book, often in perpetuity. Once you sign a contract to publish your book, your book essentially belongs to the publisher and may belong to the publisher for the lifetime of the book's copyright. This copyright lasts for the lifetime of the author and 60 years after his lifetime.

This is a really big and disappointing point. That is, if the author is not satisfied with the services of his traditional publisher, he cannot get his book republished from any other publisher at any cost. If the author republishes his book from another publisher, he may have to pay compensation. Moreover, many times most traditional publishers do not give any advance to the new author, and give only 7% to 15% of the maximum selling price as royalty.

Know well that most traditional publishers give a maximum royalty of 10%. Even if a traditional publisher agrees to publish a new author's book for the first time, it still takes a very long time for the book to hit the market, at least six months or even years.

Every stage of book publishing, such as proof-reading, editing, interior designing and cover designing, takes months to complete by a large traditional publisher. If a author does not have patience then their working method can be extremely frustrating for such authors.

Self Publishing Model

In the self-publishing model, publishers provide publishing

services to the author by taking payment, such publishers are called self-publishers. Often in the self-publishing model, the author's book is published within 15 days to a month. Often, under the self-publishing model, no publisher rejects the author's manuscript, because it is the author's right to get his work published in book form by paying a fee. Self-publishing publishers do not publish books considering the author's profile and followers, rather they provide every possible assistance to the author to fulfill his dream of book publishing, but on a paid basis.

Whereas, under the self-publishing model, the author retains all the rights related to the book, because the author is spending money to publish his book. Authors can make their own decisions about everything from book cover design to marketing, meaning authors are no longer mere puppets in the hands of a publisher. In this way, in self-publishing model, the author also receives royalty on weekly, monthly or quarterly basis for publishing the book.

Benefits of self publishing

The biggest advantage of self-publishing is that keeping in mind the author's fame or his readership or his profile, the author's manuscript is not rejected for publication. Self publishers are always ready to provide paid publication to all new or published authors. That is, the author never faces disappointment for the publication of his book.

Through the self-publishing model, the author's book is published in just a month. Due to which authors do not have to wait for many years like traditional publishing. In self-publishing, authors are free to take all decisions related to their book. This means that authors are free to decide their book's title, design, marketing, and everything else themselves. Whereas in traditional publishing the author does not have any rights.

Under the self-publishing model, all copyrights of the author's book remain with the author. Its advantage is that if the author is not satisfied with his current publisher, he can get his book published by another publisher without any permission. Whereas in the traditional publishing model, the publisher retains all the rights of the author's book.

Under the self-publishing model, the author receives higher royalties than traditional publishing and royalty payments range from weekly to quarterly basis. Also, the author himself can take the marketing plan of his book, date of publication and all other important decisions. In self-publishing, the author can decide the maximum selling price (MRP) of the book according to his profit.

The biggest disadvantage of the self-publishing model is that the author has to bear the publishing expenses himself to publish his book. Which most of the authors do not find convenient, due to which most of the authors are not able to get their book published throughout their life. While it is also noteworthy that traditional publishers do not consider his book worthy of publishing. In self publishing the author has to pay a fee for each work of the book or they can take a package as per their budget.

Under the self-publishing model, due to the facility of distribution only on online eCommerce, the author's book is likely to get very few readers. Due to which the author himself has to search for readers for his book and also has to do marketing and promotion at his own level. Whereas many self-publishing publishers also provide the facility of offline distribution, for which the author has to pay additional charges. But this is a point to be kept in mind that even after offline distribution, there is no guarantee of sales of the book and also the facility of offline distribution is for a fixed period of time, after that the author's book is no longer available offline. The conclusion is that self-published authors have to work hard at the ground level for the success of their book.

It is also a disappointing point that authors published through the traditional model mislead self-published authors by saying that self-published authors have no recognition. Due to which self-published authors do not consider themselves a respected author and try to publish their book traditionally. Due to their continuous failure, such authors start considering the self-publishing model as illegal. Whereas self publishing is a legal business model and a self published author is also a recognized author.

It is noteworthy that publishers providing self-publishing services register their publishing houses under Indian Business Acts and Companies Acts. For which no objection is raised by the Government of India, because providing self-publishing services is not an illegal business model.

Chapter 13

What is 100% royalty and how is it determined?

It remains a common misconception among most authors that the author should get 100% royalty on the Maximum Selling Price (MRP) of the book. But according to the perception of most authors, royalty is as follows; 100% Royalty = Maximum Selling Price (MRP) of the book, that is, if the Maximum Selling Price

(MRP) of the book is Rs 100 then the author should get only Rs 100 as 100% royalty. Whereas let me tell you that this concept of royalty is completely imaginary.

To satisfy your curiosity, I would like to tell you that no publisher in the world can give 100% royalty to the author as per this imaginary assumption. Having worked in the publishing industry for many years, it has been my experience that most of the authors still consider this imaginary notion to be true and keep searching for a publisher who will pay them 100% royalty as per their imaginary notion. But it is a reality that they are unable to find such publishers, due to which their books often remain unpublished for long periods of time.

Confusion about 100% royalty

Generally, new authors as well as senior literary authors remain confused that some publishers are giving 100% royalty, while many publishers give 50% or 70% royalty. There are some publishers who are offering only 10% royalty on the maximum selling price (MRP). Whereas authors do not try to know whether the publisher is paying them royalty on Maximum Selling Price (MRP) or on net profit. Ask your publisher whether the author is being paid 100% or 70% or 50% royalty on the Maximum Selling Price (MRP), or on the net profit made from the sale of each book.

How are royalties determined?

Let us explain to you how 100% royalty is determined. The

amount that remains after deducting the cost from the MRP of the book to the print cost of the book till distribution is called 100% Net Profit or 100% Royalty. i.e. 100% Royalty = MRP of the book − (Printing Cost of the book + Distribution Charges + Branded packaging cost of the ecommerce store + Taxes + Selling fees of the ecommerce company + Additional local and maintenance expenses). In this way, after deducting all the above expenses from the MRP of any book sold by any self publisher, the remainder is called 100% Net Profit or Royalty. This remaining profit or royalty is given to the author as 100% royalty. Now you must have understood that how your publisher is giving you 100% or 70% or 50% Royalty, Net Profit or Fixed Royalty on MRP.

If you choose the option of fixed royalty on Maximum Selling Price (MRP). So this can be beneficial for you, because 100% royalty can be more or less due to fluctuations in the prices of resources related to book publishing. Whereas in the fixed royalty option you will always get assured royalty. Resources related to book publishing such as paper rate, selling fees, packaging material and other small expenses which may increase or decrease over time. However, it is also noteworthy that in the last 4-5 years, the price of paper used in books, the price of packaging material and courier charges have continuously increased. For example, take a copier paper, which used to be available for just Rs 130 six years ago, which is now available for Rs 300. This is the reason that the cost of book publishing has increased significantly in the last 4-5 years, due to which all the publishers have made a lot of changes in the 100% royalty till now.

It is also a point to be noted that some publishers pay royalty by deducting tax from the royalty. Some publishers also charge to withdraw the royalties. Due to many such hidden charges which are often not disclosed to the author, the 100% royalty of the author gets reduced. That is, you can assume that there is nothing fixed under 100% royalty, whereas the assured royalty on maximum selling price (MRP) is the royalty fixed by the publisher, given to the author, because there is no fluctuation or any Tax is not levied on author's royalties.

Often authors complain that our publisher is not paying royalty on time or is paying less royalty or is not sharing the sales report of the book. To avoid facing such a situation, every author must read the publishing contract before publishing the book. Also ask the publisher to mention the royalty payment deadline and royalty clearly in numbers and words, so that one does not have to face any problem in future. It is also worth noting that no matter what the business or publishing house is, it becomes successful only through transparency and better services. Publishing houses often go bankrupt, not because of poor services and opaqueness, but because of negligence and failure to live up to the expectations of their customers.

Tips to get more royalties

Even after reading this article, you should get 100% of the selling price of the book as royalty. So in such a situation, the only advice I can give to authors is that you should get your book designed from a local DTP operator. After the design and layout work is completed, get it printed from a local printer and sell the book at your own level. In this way, by selling the book at your level, you will get 100% profit on the maximum selling price (MRP) in the form of royalty. This is also true, if you print and sell it yourself, there will be no middleman in between, you will get all your profit.

In the end, you must also know that if the publisher starts giving 100% royalty as per the imaginary notion of the author, then the publishing industry will be on the verge of closure and many publishing houses will die. Due to which thousands of jobs will be lost, which are being provided by these publishing houses.

Misconceptions Among Authors about the Publishing Industry

In our country, more awareness can be seen about freebies and discounts or one free product or one free service. Authors want the same thing in the self-publishing industry, even though they know they have to pay a fee to self-publish their book. Even after this, authors request self-publishing companies to publish the book for free. Whereas such authors feel disappointed due to not getting the facility of free book publishing from self-publishing companies. In this chapter I am presenting some information for all the authors, it will prove beneficial for you. Besides, the authors will also be able to get answers to many of your questions in this article, which you have not been able to find anywhere else.

It is well known that a doctor charges fees for his advice, lawyers charge fees for their advice, schools charge fees for teaching work, barbers charge for cutting hair and restaurants charge for their service. Also, all types of businesses in the country are charging for their services, so why shouldn't a publisher providing self-publishing services charge for its services? Whereas the publisher designs the author's book, communicates with the author, devotes time to the proof of the book, prints the books, and prints them again when the stock runs out. Makes the author's books available to the readers on online eCommerce websites and apart from this, it provides a publishing consultant team which is always ready to serve the author to provide support and updates to the author.

Funding for running the publication

Have you ever wondered whether books are printed for free? Is paper for books available free of charge? Does the publisher's staff render their services without salary? Is the electricity bill not received in the publisher's office? Doesn't the publisher's telephone and broadband bills also come? Apart from this, everyone knows the answer to these questions about how much is spent in running any office or institution in a month, because self-publishing is also a business model.

Advocates of free book publishing may indicate whether the self-publishing or traditional publisher receives any funding from the government, grants from any other voluntary organization, or non-government funding. So that the publisher provides free publishing services. I don't think being a publisher means burning down your house and watching the show. Self publishers are offering their services to get financial benefits, if you do not want to do self publishing by paying fees, then you can contact a traditional publisher. It is also worth noting that no self-publisher comes to you and requests you to publish the book by paying a fee.

If every publisher started providing free publishing services to every author, then my own guess is that the self-publishing industry would collapse, because if anyone got any facility for free, then there would be no point in There is no importance, nor does the author understand the importance of the free service or product.

Note that after the closure of the self-publishing industry, only the big publishers will continue to dominate. Which will provide an opportunity to be published only to the already established authors, which is happening even today and the rest of the authors who are self-publishing will be able to get their books printed from local printers and keep them on the shelves of their homes. .

Free Publishing and My Experience

Let me tell you my experience, my self-publishing house had published books of some authors for free in the beginning of its establishment. As a result, the authors published for free started considering themselves as very established authors and started making a lot of demands including royalties, author's copies etc. From what those authors said, I realized that perhaps books would sell well under their name, that is why they were making such big claims and demanding more.

The biggest thing is that till date he has not even shared about his book on social media, nor has he discussed about his book with anyone, because he got the free service without any major effort, which It has no importance or consider it as charity. Even if someone provides me a free service, I too might not understand its importance, because a free facility has no importance. But if I pay for the service, it will probably be too expensive for me. I will understand the importance of paid service.

Due to the incident of free publishing, I saw the saying 'Dhaak Ke Do Paat' being true, till date only two to three copies of the books published by those authors have been sold. Also, let me tell you that the stock of books printed by my publication has become waste today. I can say with guarantee that if we had continued to provide free service, we would probably have had to stop our publication. Apart from me, I have seen many publications closing down in my journey in the publishing industry, most of which have closed down for providing free publishing services.

Suppose if any traditional publisher takes up the responsibility of publishing the book of every author in the country for free. I can say with a guarantee that then any publisher will soon be declared bankrupt, because due to social media being widely available, at present a litterateur or author has been born in every street and locality of even the smallest city of the country. Most of the authors wish that their book should be published free of cost through traditional publishing medium.

This is 100% true and it is also my experience that if any author's book is published for free, then that author will promote his book for a maximum of a week only. After that he will forget that any of his books has even been published, because after this the author finds promoting his book a very boring task. The author thinks that now the book has been published and if it sells, he will definitely get royalty. Even if it doesn't sell, it won't matter to me, because I haven't spent anything. Many times a author is only concerned with getting the book published, whether it sells or not, because they just want the status of being a published author.

This is why traditional publishers, like cream from milk, select only those authors who are already established, or whose name is enough to sell the book. So that the future of their publishing house remains intact, that is, the publication does not reach the verge of closure and apart from this, the employment of thousands of people associated with the supply chain including the publishing house continues.

How long can a business offer free services?

Think for yourself, whether you are also doing a job or business, have you ever worked for anyone for free? If you are employed then you might find it a very boring task to work overtime without pay, whereas if you are doing business then you cannot even give a toffee to any customer without getting any profit.

Similarly, be it a traditional publisher or a self-publishing publisher, in both business models, publishers also have the right to think about their economic benefits. They have to pay salaries to their staff, electricity bills, internet bills and many other expenses. Which often happens in all businesses, along with this, continuous investment has to be made to maintain the publishing business.

After incurring so many expenses, you may wonder how long you can work for someone for free without any profit. Imagine if you are working in an organization, if that organization has no source of income left, will you be able to get salary or employment? The answer is – no. You will have to look for another job.

Similarly, before publishing for free, the traditional publisher also first looks at his own profit and observes whether the book of the concerned author will be sold on the basis of its content or according to the profile of the author or not. Only after that he invests lakhs of rupees on the author's book, because traditional publishers also have to make continuous investments to keep their business afloat.

Suppose you are sick and you go to the doctor and say that I am sick and treat me free of cost, because it is my right to live. Tell me will the doctor treat you free of cost? You must have often seen that the patient is not admitted to the hospital until the money is deposited at the cash counter of the hospital. While survival is the right of all of us, yet treatment facilities are available only when the hospital receives its fees. Even if the patient loses his life.

Similarly, you must have noticed that even in the education business, you deposit the fees prescribed by the educational institutions and apart from this, you deposit tuition fees separately. But here you will not stand up for your right to education, because you cannot do anything here. Here you will have to pay fees under any circumstances, otherwise you will not take education. Often parents protest against the ever increasing school fees, but even after this nothing happens. School organizations have a say in how to pay the salaries of their staff and in times of inflation they need funds to run the schools. Due to which the fees are being increased.

You must have noticed that once upon a time the consultation fee of doctors used to be fifty rupees, but now for just one visit it is necessary to get a receipt of thousand rupees, only then one can meet the doctor. Otherwise, even if your condition is very critical, you will not be given time to meet the doctor. This dilemma is present in all those areas which are necessary for our living. Not just school or doctor, a fixed payment has to be made for every item of daily life or every facility necessary for living.

Now just imagine, why shouldn't the publishing industry charge fees to survive? Do the employees working in publishing houses not have the right to receive salary for living? Rest, think for yourself whether the publishing industry is right or wrong for authors.

Do you know that thousands of poor and destitute families in the country find it difficult to get even one meal a day? Do such families not have the right to eat bread? Some people will boast of their wisdom and say that the poor should struggle and work hard to improve their lives.

I want to ask this question, if such poor and helpless families can be advised to struggle and work hard, then why do authors want to achieve success by publishing books for free? Why don't authors want to work hard for their own success? Why do authors want to rely on a publisher to succeed? Why don't authors want to take risks?

What I mean to say is that whether it is a grocer's shop, a confectioner's shop, or advocacy, or medicine, or educational institute, any other legitimate business, which also includes self-publishing companies. The aim of all these is to expand the business and earn profit. No one can provide free services in the world without profit, because providing services for free or without any economic benefit is the first condition for any business to go bankrupt.

This way you pay for every need in your life, so why not pay for your success? While the book is also yours, the success of the book will also be yours. Your book will always be yours. Keep in mind that if your book becomes successful then you will get its next edition published by making a deal with the new publisher for higher royalties, because if you become successful then you look for new opportunities. Also keep in mind that everyone always keeps their doors open for a successful person, so that others can also take advantage of his success for their own benefit.

Often some writers say on social media forums that we have to unite against the publishers, only then our books will be published free of cost. I want to ask such writers whether the publisher has any treasure? So that the authors' books can be published free of cost. I want to say to such writers that education and health is a field which should be free, for this you can unite, because donations or cooperation can be taken from the society for education and service. Whereas everyone will donate for these works without any hesitation. So that every helpless person in the country can get education and health facilities, but what donation or contribution can be given to the publishers?

Have you thought that if all the authors unite, but will the publishers publish the books of the united authors for free? The answer is that no publisher will publish the book. It is worth noting that they will never publish books by authors who are united, because they will only publish well-known authors and celebrities, famous faces of politics, social media stars. Also keep this thing in your mind that well-known and celebrity authors will not have any interest in uniting with you, because their books are being published easily without any protest or struggle.

It is also noteworthy that such writers who come together or vent against publishers on social media are those writers who do not want to take risks and want to succeed without any effort.

confusion of low or high royalties

Often authors say that publishers are paying less royalty, in such a situation I give only one advice to the authors that you should get the books printed from a local printer and sell them at your own level. You will get full profit by selling from your level. This is also true, there will be no middleman in this, the author will receive all the profit. I have told this in the previous chapter also. Often authors say that you are the one taking such huge profits, but you are giving us very little royalty. I want to tell you that the cost of each book is higher in print on demand.

Not only this, a publisher has to purchase branded packaging material from Amazon or Flipkart at his own expense. Besides, the publisher also has to pay the selling fees of Amazon and Flipkart, the fees for printing, distribution and services to other associate partners. Keeping all these things in mind, our publishing house clearly refuses the authors and tells them that we will not be able to live up to your expectations, hence we are unable to publish your book. Because earning money by making false promises is not included in the policy of our publication, nor will it ever be done in future.

A author should also know that often many readers order books from Amazon or Flipkart and return the books after a day or two citing shortcomings, now who will compensate for this loss? Obviously, the publisher or its printing or distribution or other associate partners will compensate for the loss at their own level, no compensation is sought from the author. When the book comes back, first the reader and then the courier pack the book so badly that it gets torn, who can understand this better than us.

In such cases, there is no hearing of the publisher or seller on Amazon and Flipkart, because their own customers are important for them. It does not matter to the book seller or the book publisher whether they suffer loss.

Cheapest Self Publishing Services & author expectations

If an author chooses to publish a book through a self-publisher, often all authors want is the cheapest package. Also, the demand for facilities of such authors costs lakhs. Many authors want paid promotion or marketing in a cheap publishing plan, which requires an investment of at least thirty to fifty thousand. The author does not want to make this investment, but wants it free from the publisher. You should keep in mind that the author will also have to work hard, only then you will be able to achieve success. Keep in mind that till date no one has achieved any success just by thinking.

Even if the author spends money, there is no guarantee of the result, because no guarantee is given by the advertising or marketing agency, then how can the publisher give guarantee to the author. No publisher or seller can give a guarantee even for guaranteed sales, because the reader cannot be pressurized to buy, this is discussed further.

Some authors want at least fifty percent royalty on the price of the book, which is not possible because in the print on demand or inventory management model, any publisher works as a chain with multiple printing, distribution and other collaboration partners. This has to be done so that the author's book never remains out of stock. Due to which printing and collaboration partner also share in the total cost. Also, some authors, apart from more copies, make many other demands which increase the cost, but the authors do not want to pay the cost for it.

Guaranteed to become a best-selling author, but how?

Often I talk to many authors and they say that you can make us a best seller author, then I will pay you as per your publishing plan and mail my manuscript today. To many such authors, I clearly say that we will not be able to publish your book. I also tell them that we can make the layout of your book, do editing, proof reading, get it printed and published and we can guarantee that as long as you keep your self publishing contract with us, Till then the author's book will not remain out of stock. But we cannot give you false consolation of becoming a best seller author.

Let me tell you that not only our publication, no publisher in the world can make you a best seller author, unless you work hard for the success of your book or make a promotion or marketing strategy. Otherwise you will have to make a big budget for marketing your book, only then your book can be successful.

If you really want to become a best-selling author, you will have to work on the promotion of your book like an obsession, spend money and devote most of the time to marketing your book.

The way any businessman works day and night for his business, just as a player focuses only on his target, in cricket a bowler focuses on the wicket, a batsman focuses on the ball, in the same way your focus should be on Must be on becoming a best seller author. Only through your efforts you can become a best seller author and will be able to sell more books.

Why only authors, when we also advertise our publishing house, our advertising service provider does not guarantee us that new authors will join you and get your book published. Similarly, if you are paying a fee to a publisher for marketing or promotion, it must be mentioned in their policy that payment does not guarantee that you will get results. Therefore, my advice is that to become a best seller, instead of relying on illusion and show off, work hard at the ground level.

Is paid book publishing illegal or illegal?

Many authors often contact us and mostly ask why are you taking money for book publishing? Our simple answer is that our publishing house is self publishing business model, you have to pay for each of our services. Some authors say that you people have made book publishing a money-making business, then my answer is that absolutely yes! This is a business model which is universally accepted. Publishing a book by taking money from the author is not an illegal activity or black market activity or illegal business model.

It is noteworthy that self-publishing is a widely accepted business model all over the world. The self-publishing business model has not been blacklisted or categorized as an illegal activity by the government of any country in the world.

Whereas in the self-publishing model, the publisher provides services to the author by quoting a fixed charge for all the services related to book publishing, and does not work illegally or by taking money from under the table. Whatever charge is there for publishing the book, it is in front of the author. If the charge for the services is within the author's budget then the services can be availed. Even if the author does not avail our services, the author is not harassed by repeated calls from our publication.

Buy and read books, support the author

In the end, I would like to tell the authors and readers that many authors often say that our relatives and friends ask for free copies and I am unable to refuse. Due to which, apart from the expenses of self-publishing, now a lot of expenses will be incurred in distribution. In such a case, I would like to advise the authors to explain to their friends and relatives that for success in my writing career, first of all the support of our acquaintances and friends is necessary. If our friends or acquaintances do not support us or do not tell others about the book of their friend author, then how will we get support in his writing, so please give everyone's support and blessings.

If a reader will not buy the book then how will a author be motivated, because if the books are not sold then the author will not even get royalty. Due to which the morale of the author starts falling and he moves towards stopping his writing. If you are a reader then buy your friend author's book and inspire your friends to buy the book, share it on social media. Even if you are not buying your friend's author's book, then at least share it in your friend group. So that readers' awareness of your author friend's book increases and the morale of your author friend also increases.

Chapter 15

Book Marketing Ideas for Self Published Authors

The problem that new self-published authors often face is how to market their book? Or how to reach the readers? Many times new authors are not aware of how to promote their book. In this chapter, I have tried to share some tips and information which can prove beneficial for the promotion of your book. There are just a few tips here, but you should also do some real hard work and do your own research on new marketing and promotion plans. So that we can write a new chapter for the success of your book.

Offer free copies of the book at public places

Often self-published authors distribute their copies to their acquaintances and friends, so that they know that you have published your book. This is a good effort of publicity, but often our acquaintances are not interested in books or do not have time to read. Keeping such circumstances in mind, you can do effective advertising for free by donating your books to people who are interested in reading or at public places. For example, you can gift books at prominent places like doctor's clinics, hair salons, or any place where waiting rooms are established, orphanages, old age homes, local libraries, senior centers, rehabilitation centers, because at such public places you will find readers. There is a possibility that they might like your book and consider buying your next book or search on Google for your next book. It is also possible that they may discuss your book with other acquaintances. With this you will get promotion benefits without investment. This way you can get new readers and will also get free promotion medium.

Request reviews from readers

A large number of reviews on any book attracts new readers a lot. A survey by BookBub.com, a platform for global authors, found that when a book has at least 150 reviews on Amazon or Goodreads, clicks to the book's page increase by an average of 14%. Therefore, always encourage your readers to give reviews through social media.

Request reviews from your friends and acquaintances

Authors are often hesitant to ask friends or relatives to provide reviews, but doing so can be extremely effective for marketing your book. There is nothing wrong in requesting reviews on your book, as an author it is your right to request reviews. Also make sure that your friends or relatives actually take the time to read your book, as conscious readers are well aware of fake reviews. Also, carefully check the review policies of the websites where you are requesting to post a review. For example, Amazon has strict rules for having family members review your book.

Submit your books for editorial reviews

Presently in the time of internet revolution, there are many online websites like Buuks2Read, Book Geeks, Indian Book Critics, which only publish information, reviews and articles related to books and authors. You can send your books to the editors of such websites for their book reviews. Note that many websites publish paid book reviews.

Don't forget to thank readers for their reviews

An author should always keep reading the reviews given by readers on his book, because readers not only provide free market research, but readers act like a networking tool for your book. As soon as a review is posted on your book, be sure to thank readers for their review by posting a comment on the review or sharing it on social media. This personal approach to connecting with readers leaves a lasting impression and helps generate potential buyers for your next book.

Create your author page on Amazon

Create your Author Page on Amazon and upload your professional looking photo and well presented Author Bio. Your Author Page will look a little blank until the number of your published books increases.

Create an Author Fan Club

Fan Clubs are groups where all readers can gather without the expectation of helping with promotional activities. Readers or fans can interact directly with authors, discuss books, and chat about books with like-minded readers.

Advertise your previous books in the new book

It can be a good option for authors to advertise their previously published books in a page on the back of their new books. This is usually just one page, containing the book's title, description, cover image, and website address to purchase. This may inspire the reader to buy the author's old books.

Publish Multi-author Anthology

Publish a collection of articles or short stories or poems

and partner with other established authors. If you promote an anthology to your readers and other authors to their readers, you can increase your readership by reaching the readers of other authors included in your anthology. Many times authors do not want to take paid participation in shared collections, as I have mentioned earlier that the mentality of such authors is that they have the right to publish for free.

Organize Readers Interviews from time to time

A author should always take care of his readers. For this, you should do a small interview with your readers from time to time and share it on your social media handle, so that the readers can connect with you emotionally. You can also share the experiences of your readers on your social media accounts.

Contact Local Book Stores

Often the owners of local or established book stores in your city are interested in selling books by local authors, so contact local book stores and talk to them about selling your book through them, because unless you start on your own, Till then no one will come to you and give you an offer. If you know other local authors, get them involved too and don't forget to bring your signed copies.

Create a YouTube Channel

Like podcasting, video posts are becoming increasingly popular and can cover just about every topic you can think of.

You can also create a YouTube Channel where you can talk about your book, read excerpts from the book, post interviews of other authors, answer reader/viewer questions. For example, you could create a video slideshow of your book reading. In the notes to the video, write a paragraph or two about yourself and your book, and then link to where readers can purchase your book online.

Sell your book to libraries

Did you know that libraries sometimes buy books from independent authors too? Just make sure your books are available through a wholesale bookseller or publisher, as most libraries will not purchase books without an invoice. Contact your local library and make an effective presentation about your book and why they should stock your book in their library. Once your book is available in one library, it becomes easier to bring it to more libraries.

Advertise on Facebook

If you can afford to spend a small amount of money promoting your book, write a Facebook post as if it were an advertisement for your book, including an eye-catching photo. Post it on your Facebook account or page. Apart from this, you can also share this post on any social media websites or groups of your choice. More importantly, you can also do paid promotion from your Facebook Page. You can do this very inexpensively, and it's a great option for reaching new readers.

Join Facebook Groups

Join Facebook groups related to books and readers. Where you can promote your book and also introduce yourself. Don't promote the book right away in the first place. This may also have a bad effect on readers or other group members.

Advertise through Google Ads

Advertise on Google Ads with target keywords that your readers are most likely to search for books like yours. Create multiple versions of ad copy in each ad group and let Google automatically run each variation and determine targeting. For better results, you can also take the help of an experienced marketing agency. I would advise you to take the help of an experienced marketing agency for the promotion of your book, so that you can get better results, because if you try to set up the advertisement yourself then you may be likely to make mistakes. Due to which you may suffer financial loss. Whereas the marketing agency has good experience in running advertisements.

Take part in contemporary interviews

Try to participate in contemporary interviews where you can effectively reach the target readers. Authors should take advantage of such opportunities to brand themselves and increase awareness of their books. Participate actively in public forums and request organizers to discuss your book on the forum. Apart from this, also distribute some copies of the book for free.

Consider what you really need

The big question is what kind of results you want to get from your book. Most book promotion companies are very clear about what results they are going to give you. If you are hiring an experienced book promotion company to promote your book, be sure to understand what results you want and get this in writing from the promotion company before you start working with them.

Consider Sales Expectations

This is especially true if the book you are publishing is your first book. Selling books takes time and most book promotion companies will tell you the same thing. Most books do not start selling immediately, books require a lot of time and promotion budget. So it is important that you plan your book promotion budget and your book marketing accordingly. Don't spend your entire marketing budget straight away and if you make sure you spend it the right way, making the right decisions, you can achieve your goal.

Run Targeted Social Media Ads

Social media websites like Facebook and Twitter give you the option to target ads to targeted audiences based on preferences expressed by users on their platforms. This allows you to advertise your book to people interested in similar books or genres to yours. You can advertise on Facebook as per your budget as compared to Twitter. You can run ads on Facebook with a budget of at least

Rs 100 per day and on Google with a budget of at least Rs 200 per day. Whereas Twitter requires more budget than both of these websites. Services of an experienced marketing agency can also be taken to run advertisements on social media. Note that marketing agencies charge you as per your requirement and target.

Write and Syndicate a Press Release

Create an informative press release announcing the publication of a new book. Link to online books and link to your website keeping SEO in mind. Use a Free Press Release Distribution to syndicate press releases to news websites and blogs. Some major websites include Free Press Release Distribution, Issue Wire, PRZoom, OpenPR, Prnewswire, Betanews, Einpresswire, Presswire, Onlywire etc., where you can submit press releases.

Contact local news agencies

Send press releases to local media websites giving your book's release information and also drop off a free copy at their office. Request publication by sending a press release and personal letter along with the book. Local media generally give priority to local news. Get a little information about your regional media offices or find your local media outlet. Also send them an introductory email to confirm that you are a local author and that news about your book could be of value to their newspaper.

Run a contest for readers

Run a contest to get readers to share your post, comment on a post, or like a post, and offer a free signed copy of a book or other enticing prize as a prize. Promote the contest on your other social media channels.

Share the link of your new book

Find a high-visibility place to link to your book. As such, many authors include a link to the book in their personal email signature, Twitter Bio, Facebook Page Bio, About Me Page, and Linkedin Bio. Which works as advertisement for authors.

Keep your book prices low

Readers today have millions of book purchasing options, so it's a good idea to give new readers the option of a low-cost book so they can get to know you. This is also a great strategy for you if you are publishing a book for the first time. Often many authors set the price of their book too high in the first edition, due to which their books do not sell and they move away from potential readers.

Claim your Social Media Profile

Be sure to create your page or profile on Facebook, Twitter, Instagram, Pinterest, Tumblr, LinkedIn, and About.me. Even if you don't have active profiles on every site, at least register your name and inform readers who visit your most active social media profiles.

Create a Goodreads Profile

Goodreads is a huge social network of readers. Goodreads is a place where people go to share what they are reading and while Goodreads is known for making the careers of many authors. Therefore, you must create your profile on Goodreads and claim your profile.

Make sure to get an author website

An author must create his own author website. Where information about the author, books and links to buy the book should be available. Also keep in mind that your site should be a marketing tool that serves as the hub for all your online activities, from blogging to selling books to sending newsletter emails. Make sure to create a page linking to all your books on your website.

Make books available for pre-order

Run pre-order and notify readers before publishing your book. So that you can know the estimated sales and readership trends. This also has the advantage that your readers can share the link and discuss with others after pre-order.

Survey your target readers

Survey potential readers of the book about demographics, psycho-graphics and behavior. So that you can better understand how to attract readers and which of your posts or messages they are most likely to respond to. After the survey, as per the choice of the readers, post some excerpts of the book on social media from time to time, so that the readers can share and comment, so that you can get new readers.

Offer free copies to top Amazon reviewers

One of the best options for getting reviews for your new book is to offer a free copy to reviewers of any of your previous books and reach out with a polite request. If you are a first-time author, you can check out Amazon's Top Reviewers and shortlist the people you want to review your books. However, Amazon does not support reviews for pre-order books. If you've released a paperback version of your book and linked it to your unpublished ebook, any reviews posted for the paperback will be copied to your ebook. This way, your book will be ready with social proof the day it launches. Goodreads allows reviews to be posted for pre-release books. Note that even though Goodreads is owned by Amazon, reviews posted on one site cannot be migrated to another. In general, contact four times as many reviewers as you are targeting.

Send digital gifts to readers who pre-order

Sending gifts by courier or post to readers who pre-order can be an expensive option, so Digital Gift Packs can be a great option. This may include exclusive content such as short stories, author commentary, deleted scenes, or high-resolution posters.

Continue publishing new books

Often authors get disappointed when their first book is not successful, whereas they should always try new experiments to make their book reach the readers. Apart from this, new books should be published at regular intervals. So that continuously publishing new books will help you get a wider readership, the reader may be interested in your other books.

__Note:__ In this chapter, the author of the book 'How to Become a Best Seller Author' has studied many websites for marketing and promotion tips and has presented them in his writing style. Special thanks to Bookbub.com and eBookit. com and other sources for the content of this chapter.